Please note: ZMP, in most cases, only does light editing to prepare a book for publishing. The original manuscript from the author is kept intact and in the author's on words with only minimum editing.

The Night The Stars Aligned

by

Jeffrey Lilly Jr

I had no clue that when I was born the journey of my life would be filled with so damn many ups and downs. From losing my twin brother right at birth. To losing my little brother, Father, and my Mother as well before I was 50 years old. Remembering back now to the first year of my loss. It was total chaos for me. Coming so damn close to having a full-on nervous breakdown. I had to see a shrink because of all of the terrible things I'd seen during my lifetime. And was finally diagnosed with P.T.S.D. because of those same very things I had gone through during my life. So many tragic ordeals I had suffered through repeatedly. From seeing a very good friend die in a horrible car crash. To seeing two church members dying from another car crash just feet away from my home. They had just left the church parking lot when another friend of mine had came flying up the hill towards them while he was intoxicated.

He had killed them immediately upon impact And In doing so He would end up spending the next 8 years in prison for that very same accident. I had seen so much tragedy in my youth. But nothing would prepare me for what I would experience at a much later date in my life. By that time I had seen so many people that I had grown up with get severely injured and or killed.

And yet some would still survive from their horrible ordeal. I'd seen a woman stab herself in the leg as well. Right before my very own eyes. I had also seen people beaten so badly it was so unsettling. I had vomited from the smell of the blood alone. Life was nothing short of bad happenings for me and for the ones I loved. The worst tragedy I'd endured was the suicide of my Uncle Lester. Shortly after becoming a brother of the Church.

Then one night out of nowhere. The stars would all seem to align perfectly. Allowing me to witness something very few get to see in their lifetime. Something truly Majestic and yet wickedly beautiful. Which would also be life-changing and very scary for me as well. Seeing what one isn't supposed to ever see. Becomes a battle deep down inside of your soul. Trying to make true sense of it all.

During the days of my youth, I remembered back, to experiencing on so many occasions De-Ja-Vu. Even a few of my own family members had been blessed with some form of mental or spiritual gift also. Dreams would often spark rumors of a death or pregnancy coming sooner than later. My life was wild in so many ways. But I lived very wildly as well back then.

My Aunt Brenda had a special gift. She could see things coming well before they would happen. This occurred often during my teenage years. And I would have to say quite honestly that She was always spot on when she predicted something. That was the simple truth. My Grandmother had also been born with this special gift.

They could almost foresee the future at certain times. At times it would scare us to death. My friends and I would always fish every single weekend. The dreams that my Aunt and Grandmother would have. Put fear into all of us. The fear that one of us would drown or some other form of accident could possibly take place. In all honesty, their dreams and or Nightmares would keep us on our toes. Keep us from considering any type of horseplay while out camping or Night Fishing. For the most part, that scenario kept most accidents at a bare minimum. After all, it would for the most part be when I was by myself that the strange occurrences would often take place.

The first Sasquatch encounter that I ever had I always considered that one kind of a tricky one. My sister and I were on our way home from school that day. When the first sounds came crashing in as the rock smacked the pavement. I heard the loud whooping sounds. Looking back to see nothing behind us at all.

Only after the second set of whoops came in would I realize that we were in a situation. Looking over towards the woods only to see something, not of this world. Something I had been warned about but really didn't believe to be remotely true whatsoever. As the moments passed on I came to the understanding that what I was seeing was real. All of the stories that I had been told were most likely true.

This creature which stood upright at no less than 7 ½ feet tall pushing 8 feet, to be honest. Fur or hair that blew in the breeze but couldn't be distinctly pointed out from the distance other than Black with White tips. The muscles were huge and very impressive, to say the least. The shaking of the two saplings that it stood between as if they were twigs. The power this creature had was very shocking.

The bobbing and weaving of the head so fast to remain unseen. So quickly as if it were some sort of professional fighter. That was how fast this creature moved at times. Throwing rocks that only a person with super strength could throw that distance. Skin the color of a human that had a deep tan from too much sunlight. A dark tan-colored skin that matched the beast's body perfectly. It was in those few moments of time that I came to the conclusion that I had been blessed by the God's. To witness a situation of this kind. Seeing a Myth a Legend. Folklore stories rushing back into my head from the past. It was truly a sight for sore eyes. And my sister and I had been privileged enough to see this amazing creature.

Looking back on that glimpse moment in time. That I had been fortunate enough to see this creature was more than enough for me. It felt as if this amazing hybrid hominid had become lost and we had just arrived at the wrong place at the wrong time. Or the exact opposite. However one would want to view the situation.

I feel that we had just crossed a boundary that day. The Sasquatch had traveled down the railroad tracks most likely and had somehow become lost. Woods surrounded our whole city. They were thicker on the North side of town. Several parks were on the higher ground of town. An Indian burial site was located there as well. Close to where we were at that time.
So it all comes down to simple facts. Was it fate or just a freaky coincidence that had occurred? That was the only conclusion I could ever draw up or come to on this subject. It was just an overwhelming encounter. But little did I know it would just become the start of everything that I would experience during my life outdoors.
Several years would pass before the next encounter would take place. And the way that it would happen was almost as if it were a Buildup to one huge experience that would alter the course of my life from that moment forward. It would also help me to start my research on this subject as well.

In total if I had to count the total number of encounters or freak experiences I've had in my lifetime I would have to say the numbers would be roughly 6 in all. Some were more intense than others but still, any one of them had affected me somehow in some way. Your body alerts you when something is Just off or not right.

Especially when your in the woods and forests of the United States. So many stories of encounters have come to light in the past 70 years. Looking at this one can easily say that not all of these stories can be lies. It is really not possible that every single story of an encounter can simply be explained away.

Someone out there has a true story about seeing this amazing creature. I know that I can not be the only one to have ever seen this creature not only once but twice in a lifetime. So after my last encounter, I would come to terms with it at some point and let it all out. To allow my spirit to heal from the damage that had occurred.

When it comes down to it I simply have to say that aliens and Sasquatch are not combined together to create these experiences that are happening. Now extraterrestrial life forms may be just as curious as we are about this species of man. And are basically doing a different type of research other than what we are doing. We may never know.

All of these special locations where cattle and sheep, as well as goats, are being mauled and mutilated by some other form of life that is out there possibly roaming among our population of mankind. To this point there can be no explanation as to what it is exactly, that is doing what seems to be experiments on these different animals.

It is my belief that it is just a coincidence that people are encountering U.F.O. contact in or around the same locations as the Sasquatch are being encountered. I believe that the phenomenon of the two different subjects are a separate situation altogether. Even though most often people encounter both life forms while in or near the woods.

During each encounter that had happened with me. There was never any other life form present in those moments. Just myself and the Sasquatch. Sometimes maybe even more than one may have been around present at the time. I have never seen more than one Sasquatch during any encounter. Even though sometimes I did feel as if I were surrounded at a certain Point in time.

When a person has a wildlife experience their mind begins to play tricks on them. Right at the moment of contact, the brain tries to explain away the encounter. Right there in that moment. And from that point on your mind continues to try and re-create the situation over and over again. Trying to make sense of it all. That's where the doubt comes in. That's why I go back in my mind from time to time.

So many times. Hell, It took me well over twenty-plus years to come to terms with exactly what it was that I had seen that night on that small mountain top right smack on the borderline of Ohio and Indiana. We were at a perfect location for this to happen. But it had taken many years for this exact situation to unfold. This was when I realized that there was a reason I'd kept having these encounters occur.

I would have to go through what now seemed to be kind of a Buildup. As if God had planned for this to happen all along. Just as it all had unfolded perfectly. From one step to the next, it all seemed to be as if I were being educated. That is the only way I can explain it to this day. I couldn't believe this was happening to me. It would take many years to get a handle on it all, after the fact.

I will never forget my second encounter. The Lake Cowan Region. North Eastern Ohio at 8 am. We were fishing on the opposite side of the lake when my best friend had cast out his line. Accidentally running a spoon deep into my ear. We had to rush back to the bait house in order to get the spoon removed from my upper ear lobe.

After getting back to the other side of the lake and to the boat house. I had the spoon cut out of my ear by the boat housekeeper. I had bitten down on a wooden spoon as he cut the barb off of the hook with a pair of brand new sharp needle nose pliers. Finally releasing me from agony in just under a minute after arriving.

The pain slowly subsided over the next few minutes. My friend talked me into making a short trip over to a place called Todd's Creek. I would debate this for a few minutes. Deciding then to make the trip over to fish for White Bass. When we arrived I had this feeling come over me as if something huge was going to happen. I couldn't explain the feeling but it was full on rush.

I will never forget the feeling that I had that day. As we parked I looked over towards the woods. Staring at the thickness of them. Wondering if we made the right choice. Just moments ago I had been injured pretty significantly. The pain was still there but, had kind of dulled down a little bit. The excitement was now building inside of me taking over.

We got out of the truck and made the long walk towards the deep part of the creek. There we would have the best chance to catch a big fish or two. The walk took several minutes time in all. The walk-in total was well over 5 hundred yards long. Really pushing 6 hundred yards in all to be honest. It was one hell of a walk.

When we finally arrived we looked down the small embankment and into the creek. The water was so clear that day. You could see straight to the bottom of the creek. The waterfall was so beautiful the crystal clear Blue water poured over and down into the bottom running into the creek. The woods fully encircle the whole area for miles and miles.

I remember stepping down into the water that day. We hadn't brought our waders and the water was so damn cold that morning. We both only had t-shirts and shorts on. Chris immediately waded down to the mouth of the creek. As I stayed up near the waterfall. I knew that there was plenty of oxygen being stirred up as the water from its fall hit the creek and steadily flowed downstream.

I felt as if there would be more fish up near this area. Where the waterfall hit the creek. I was determined to catch the biggest fish that day. As we fished the area we caught several fish each. I was basking in the sun, my injury had finally subsided a bit as I look up suddenly to take a peek at the sky on that beautiful day.

It was in that moment as I had raised my head to look at the beautiful morning sky. When I'd heard that first Whoop, and shortly thereafter followed that first rock. It had come flying in right next to me. Only landing several feet from my legs. I immediately looked down towards my best friend. As I say to him "brother why in the hell would you throw a rock at me"?
He replied to me in an instant. "I didn't throw a rock at you". "Are you kidding" ? he says to me as I reply back. "I'm serious man, a rock just landed right next to me". But I notice he has both of his hands on his fishing rod. He then said to me. "I wouldn't throw a rock at you". "That would scare the fish brother". "Think about it" he says yet again to me.
We were both kind of dumbfounded at this point in time. We both go back to fishing and think nothing of it. But in the back of my mind, I'm already thinking if another rock comes in my way I'm out of here ASAP. Several minutes passed by as we cast a few more times each. Throwing rooster tail spinners into the creek. About ten minutes had passed by and out of nowhere here it came again. Another Whoop, then another rock, even bigger than the last one flying in. Landing even closer to me in the water. I looked down towards Chris as he is now looking up towards me. It was at that moment that we both knew something was not right at all. I felt as if we had been watched

the whole damn time. As soon as our eyes locked in on one another we took off.

Was there someone else in the woods? It was only 7:30 or 8:00 in the morning on a Saturday. Out in the middle of nowhere, miles away from any community. Who or what could this be throwing rocks at me? It was only a matter of 2 or 3 seconds that I had frozen in fear, before taking off, out of the water. My best friend was right on my ass, not to far away from me.
As fast as we could we both ripped through the creek. The waters current limiting our ability to get to the other side. Fear had totally taken over at this moment. We were both trying to get out of the creek and back to the truck. The feeling of being safe was now very much needed. As we were now both scared to death. We struggled to get up and out of the creek. The steep bank was now so wet and the mud so slippery. We both now fought to get up and out of its grasp. Constantly looking over towards the other side of the forest. Never laying eyes on whatever it was that was throwing rocks at me. But most definitely hearing something stirring about the area.
Finally making it to the top of the bank. We climbed up and out freeing ourselves from the sloppy mud that was just below us. We started to run down along the fence line. Hundreds of yards

from the truck. We could see the truck but it looked as if it were so far away. The thought was that we would never make it in time. Possibly being killed before getting to the truck was my feeling.

We struggled to get moving, our clothes were now soaking wet from the creek water that we had run through. As we approached the halfway point. We started to hear a pack of dogs barking loudly. As they seemed to be chasing something suddenly out of nowhere. There seemed to be a chase on at that time. Trees and twigs could be heard breaking and snapping as there was a situation happening in the woods.

That to us had confirmed something must have been out there and over just on the other side of the woods. The goal now was to just make it to the truck and get out of the area. Safe once again from harm's way. We looked over at each other. Both of us saying at the same time. That can't be a coon they are chasing. We both knew that coons were hunted at night time.

It was at that moment I knew I had just had another encounter with a Sasquatch. No one else could have been there that morning. So far out and away from civilization. That early in the day. We both knew it as we raced towards the truck. The sounds were quite loud now. The snapping of branches and the ruffling of the brush. When we finally had arrived at the back of the truck. We stopped and immediately threw the poles in the back. As we jump in the truck Chris struggled to grab his keys from his pockets. The fear had overwhelmed him. As he pulled the Keys he tried to slide them into the ignition. Not being able to do so, I grabbed the keys and put them in the ignition, and turned the key over, starting the truck instantly. As I yelled at him to go right now.

We peeled out, the tires spinning flinging dirt all about. We turned around and got out of the area. Never to fish there again. We talked about what had happened and knew in the end we had an encounter with a Sasquatch. There was no doubt about it. We stopped fishing for quite a while after that ordeal. It had changed us, we both now had a fear of the woods. And that was a fact.

After about a year of abstaining from fishing altogether. We finally decided to go on a trip down on route 32. The Beechmont Levy. We had not fished there in a long time. It was a spot that others had fished on a regular basis. So we decided to not fish there for a while. To allow the fish numbers to grow once again. Before going back there too fish once again.

Upon arriving we had ran into a group of friends that we had grown up with in our hometown. Immediately we were told about a so-called wild man that had been running about the area. Scaring people and running them out of the woods. We were hesitant on going down and into our regular spot. We had just gone through a wild encounter ourselves not long ago. And we both knew something was off for sure about the whole situation as of late.

It was so far down to our fishing spot. That we felt as if we'd be trapped. If we went that deep into the woods and had made actual contact with one of these things. Weighing our options out, we finally decided to make the trip down after going through all of the necessary preparations we had to go through to get to this point.

The two of us had both decided to continue. And made the walk down and felt as if eyes were on us the whole damn time. It was a very unpleasant feeling and we both had that feeling once again. We decided to push on forward why? I will never be able to answer that question. We arrived and set up as fast as possible. This was another one of our great spots to fish.

I gathered as much firewood as I could for the night hours. I knew that was a very important task to take on. But I did so to make sure we could see. I knew also that the bigger the fire the less the chance of anything messing with us. I'd learned that some time back from my Uncle Jack. He had taught me almost everything he'd known about the outdoors.

Once the fire pit had been set up I started baiting poles and casting them out into the deep pools of the river. We were down on the spot known as the Slab. A huge 50 by 50 square foot piece of concrete that had been flattened out way back some time ago. It was perfect for fishing and camping. And was swarming with big fish. On this night we had decided to use fresh tiger shrimp and chicken livers for bait.

When we both finally had baited and threw all of our lines out we waited for the fish to come through and take off with our line. Night came upon us quickly. Over on the opposite side of the woods. Something was moving about frantically. Twigs and branches were being broken and snapped. It had once again caused a very unsettling feeling that had come over the two of us.

The whole situation felt off to me. But I was just living in the moment I wanted to fish. It had been quite a while since I had been out in the woods. I had missed it deeply, my connection to the woods had been locked down a very long time ago. It would take a serious tragedy to keep me from breaking that connection once and for all.

The darkness grew as the daylight slowly subsided. I started to prepare the fire so we wouldn't be in the dark. And our fishing could continue as we'd intended it to go. Right as the sun had set we started to hear it once again. The opposite side of the woods had lit up with activity once more. Something was definitely stirring about once again.

I knew in my gut something was wrong once again. As soon as it had started up the noises the sounds. Branches and limbs are being broken from off of the trees. The fire was now raging as I continued to pour on the logs. I was not allowing the fire to dwindle down to a minimum, putting us at risk. I wasn't taking any chances.

Whatever happened I had to continue to keep the fire going strong. That was our safety net. And I knew that Chris knew nothing about the situation we were in until well after the incident. About an hour later we both heard what sounded like a huge splash coming from across the river.

It was at that moment that I thought this creature had just jumped into the river and was now coming across to our side of the forest. Now I was freaking out intensely. I started to think out the scenarios. Allowing them to play out in my head. I was totally spooked at this point. I then started to debate quickly about leaving.

I felt like this thing, most likely a Sasquatch was coming to check us out. I had already experienced more than one encounter in my life. So I was educated a bit about their activity. Migration patterns as well as their diet. I had already started to do research after the Todd's Creek Incident. That's when it all started for me on an educational level.

We both heard this thing hit the bank and get out of the river. Then nothing for a few moments. I continued to pour on logs in the fire pit. I wasn't allowing this fire to die out in any way shape or form. Our lives were now on the line. I wasn't going to allow this to be my last moment on earth.

I started to really pay attention to the situation. Not allowing my fear to take over. We waited to hear each step, each sound being made. So we would know the location of whatever this was that was now stalking us. We needed to know where this thing was at. So we could manage the situation. It was either a Deer or a human. Or it was the Myth the Legend once again.

Every few seconds the creature or whatever this thing was. Would take a step closer it seemed. After a few minutes had gone by I knew it wasn't afraid of the fire. And that it was most definitely time to leave the area. I told Chris to pack it up A.S.A.P. it was time to go. He agreed immediately and started packing up.

With each second that passed, I knew we were in more danger. I could feel it in my bones. All the way to my soul to be honest. I knew we were in a bad situation. So I made a homemade torch from out of the burning fire. And we walked out of the woods backward scared for our lives. The whole time having the feeling as if we were being paralleled the whole damn time.

Feeling as if we were being followed, stalked even at times during our way out of the woods. Once we had arrived at the truck we threw the equipment in the back of the bed and got in and drove off fleeing out of the area. Never going back there again either. We were now running out of fishing spots. But we also were now growing more hip to what it was that was going on.

A period of time would go by and I wouldn't fish anywhere. I was now fully conscious of just exactly what it was that was roaming about out in the woods and forests of our country. I knew for a fact what most others had no clue about. And that in itself scared me to death. The question I asked myself now was just how many different breeds of species were their actually out there? I had done my homework at this point. And I knew of what was thought to be 4 different types of this creature. The aggressiveness varied between them. So there is no room for error when encountering these amazing creatures. They are so unpredictable we know so very little about them. Still to this day.

After I had done my research on this amazing creature. I was
ready once again to get out in the woods. Where I was at peace,
I'd spent so many years even as a Young kid camping and fishing
in the woods of Ohio. I wasn't about to let just anything scare me
away from my peace and serenity my one love in life.

The woods was where I'd always gone to sort out my life's
matters. Whether they be good or bad. It was where I sorted it
all out. That's just how it was for me. I had learned to do it long
before I was even an adult. For me, the woods and forests were a
release. Even after I had learned that I wasn't the only human-
like creature out there roaming about.
I'd learned to come to terms with it. I had made peace with the
situation. Or at least so I had thought. It wouldn't be until a few
years later that I would learn differently. I started to fish once
again. I had a yellow Ford Mercury Monarch at the time. In the
back sat about 1,000 dollars worth of gear and equipment for
fishing. Poles a tent and waders as well as a couple of lanterns.
I really shelled out lots of money on my endeavors. I fished the
Newtown Ohio area quite often and the local lakes as well. There
were big fish to be had all about Ohio. If you knew the right
spots. I had fished with so many others. And had learned a great
deal about when and where to fish. I had learned and picked up

so many important tips from my Uncle.

My problem was that I had grown a custom for night fishing. And sure enough, that was also when most encounters occurred with these creatures. So I started off on a bad foot so one could say. I wasn't too far out and that was actually the scariest part of it all. Most people have had encounters while close to their homes. That was what really had me scared. Out of curiosity, they would creep in close on people's homes, often taking food from their garbage. These creatures had learned how to survive, whatever it took would be done. They apparently had evolved over time. And now weren't too afraid of coming in close to grab food or even people's garbage in order to survive.

This would become so true. Looking back to the past there were so many encounters and sightings back in the 1990's it was insanity. The Chaos and Mayhem that had gone on with these encounters. Stories of many Sasquatch being hit by cars. Shot at as well I'd heard rumors of several Sasquatch being killed. But not too sure that was actually the case.

That was also the decade that I would have my close-up encounter with one of these Wicked yet Beautiful species of Hybrid humans so it seemed to be the case. I would go often to a spot that Noone was in. There I would set out to catch the biggest Catfish in that area at the time. Hoping to impress my friends. That's just how we did things back then.

That was what my friends and I fished for back in those days. Bass and Trout as well as Crappie also. I remember one-night fishing down along the stretch of Round Bottom Road. Newtown, Ohio. A ways from home but not too far at all only 20 minutes away. The scenery in the daytime was beautiful. At night it totally changed.

There was an inlet where 3 bodies of water collided and ran into just one huge stretch. This would be where I chose to fish. It was a stretch of woods and forest with very few houses and few and far between. That's what I wanted, away from everyone. That was where my peace and serenity came into play.

It was also a spooky place to be by yourself as well. The fog would often come rolling in a few hours after the sunset. It was thick and adequate enough to make seeing very difficult at times. But I loved being out there with nature as one a whole. That's how good it felt to be outside anywhere in or near the woods.

I can't explain it, I just felt at peace while out in the wilderness. Usually, I felt better totally alone and on my own. On this night I was alone and fishing the inlet with four poles. When the fog had started rolling in on me. It was thicker than ever on this night. I had already been there for about two hours. And I had already caught a couple of nice channel catfish over 4 pounds.

I had them in a fish basket and down in the river to keep them alive. At about 2 am a pocket of fog came rolling in from the back channel of the river. Once it had arrived I couldn't see at all. I couldn't even cast my line out. I tried patiently to wait out the fog. But it just became so damn thick and overwhelmed me very quickly.

As it grew thicker by the moment I felt as if it would soon pass by. And that I would be able to start fishing once again. But that moment never came again that night. The fog became thicker by the minute. And I started to feel as if I were being watched. I started to hear strange noises coming from the woods just the opposite of me.

Over on the point, a rock had come flying in. Crashing into the water nearby. I knew then something was near me again. As the fog became so much thicker I started to feel as if I weren't safe anymore. I packed up my gear as I started to hear sounds. A Whoop from off at a distance. Then again another Whoop that was a little closer as it carried about in the cool night air.

Totally feeling intimidated I rushed for the car. Opening up the trunk and throwing my gear inside and shutting the trunk. I got in and drove off knowing now that these creatures were all over

Ohio there was no doubt it at all in my mind. But I also knew to keep my mouth shut. Nobody would believe me. Not even for a second.

The way these encounters were all unfolding had taught me that these creatures were very timid. Very elusive and defensive creatures. They had to be in order to survive for so long. Living beside their fellow man on this earth. Looking back on all of my encounters now I've learned so much about this hybrid Hominid species.

I've watched the video of the Genome project. I've watched footage of the whole study from the very beginning to end. The higher-ups of our government are trying to keep a lid on this subject. Hoping it doesn't pop off. It will bring about mass hysteria. Those of us researchers know the extent of the damage it could cause worldwide.

That is why our powers that be in our country and others continue to keep the subject low-key. To keep the secret from the world. They suggest that it's best for the world to keep this a shut case with one another. As they do we still have many research groups all across America and other countries as well. As they push forward and continue to collect evidence by way of D.N.A. and other samples as well.

Stool samples and hair samples. Casting footprints as well as hand prints. Video footage and pictures are also being collected. Stacking up mass amounts of evidence that is needed to prove the existence of this Creature. Not to forget the audio footage of these amazing creatures talking to one another. And I've recently learned that finally, a blood sample had even been collected as well. And sent to several different labs for testing. Communicating and even howling out in the middle of the night. We've seen footage from all over the world. Ohio and Kentucky, Indiana, all the way to California, and on to Washington, and Oregon. These amazing beasts are everywhere. The estimates are anywhere from 5,000 to 65,000 in total.

The world has enough forestry and resources to accommodate a species of this form. There is plenty of enough cover and plenty of wild game and plants, and fish as well as wild berries to eat. It has been proven time and time again that there is plenty of sustenance to sustain more than several clans or more of this species.

When we look back on our past. Sometimes things that had happened come to the light. For me, it really came to light the several experiences that I had. While out fishing in different parts of Ohio. Clermont County was where I had another encounter out near the East Fork Lake Region. Right at sunset, it had happened.

I was fishing a park out in Clermont County. A stretch of the Miami River area. Around the Devil's Backbone area. Again during the nighttime hours was my choice to fish. I had arrived and set up a tent in the camping area. Walking down the trailhead shortly after arriving at the river. During this trip, the water was very low in one section.

I walked directly across the low part of the river and hit the opposite side of the bank. I wanted to fish an area that others hadn't quite fished so much as of late. I wanted to really help my chances of catching a big catfish. So I cast out my line into a pocket of deep water. Hoping to hit the honey hole. I had fished there many times before so I knew this section of water very well.

I waited patiently for a while to allow the fish that might be in the area to find the bait. But nothing even checked it out. Not A bite one at all. So I reeled my line in and went to let out another cast. Upon doing so I threw my bait towards the middle of the river. When my bait finally had hit the water. Directly beside it, something else had landed right next to it. At the same exact time.

What sounded like a rock had landed right next to my bait. It was at that moment that I totally freaked out. I was out in the middle of nowhere. I was a few hundred yards away from any other people. I was freaking out at this point. Not thinking too clearly. What was it that had just landed next to my bait?

When it happened the second time that was it for me. The only thing I remember was that it felt like I was running across the river bed as if Jesus had parted the water for me to make my way across in that moment of time. I was flying through the trail system. That was the third time that I had rocks thrown at me while fishing.

Making it back through the trails I left my friend and his girl inside as I passed them by and got into my car. I sat there weighing all of the options in my mind. I just couldn't wrap my head around all of the craziness that was going on in my life. I couldn't believe that I was having these incidents happen each and every time I went into the woods.

I already knew what it was that was toying with me. I already knew what these beasts looked like. I knew they were powerful and evasive. I knew they were also very defensive as well. They were smart as hell these creatures. And without a doubt were well adapted to their available surroundings.

After several encounters. I had only experienced one actual sighting in all at this point. That was the wild part about it all. It just goes to show you how elusive these Hybrid Hominids really are truthfully. It would be several more years down the road before I would actually see one full-on and up close. To close for comfort actually and it would be life-changing.

I remember sitting in that car all night long trying to come to terms with what exactly it was that my sister and I had seen years earlier. Just a normal trip on the way home from school. This was back in the 1980s when this had happened. Sightings were reported from all over the country that year.

Western New York, Montana, Indiana, Ohio, and quite a few other States had many reports of sightings occurring. Footprint photos, as well as a picture of a supposed Bigfoot head, were found in the Lewiston New York area. And also a picture of a huge hairy beast running for the woods. Away from an all-terrain vehicle, it had been checking out.

The Story would be written on March 3rd, 1980. By the Courier Express. The Niagara County Beast. A headline reading "Bigfoot?" Standing at 6 feet tall and weighing over 350 pounds the officer had stated. I just really don't know what to call it. Filicetti told the Courier Express.

I began researching information about Bigfoot encounters and sighting reports as my teenage years rolled around. I would have a few more incidents myself. I knew more than most skeptics that were out there ridiculing others who had seen this amazingly built creature. I wanted answers and that was that. I wanted to know why this subject was suppressed by the higher-ups. There were reports from all over the world. But what shocked me the most I believe was the sightings coming out of the New York area. Whitehall is popular for sightings. On route 4 several encounters had been reported just a half mile from one another. A 6-foot bipedal upright walking creature on two legs had popped up over a guard rail.

It had walked straight across the highway to the other side. Walking up the embankment so quickly the truck driver had reported it at 10:10 on a Monday evening. The typical report information was given. A Black hairy creature with wide shoulders and a small neck. A very impressive build mostly muscle, and a huge broad chest.

I sat in my car all night until the sun rose once again. I fell asleep off and on a few times during the night. I had exhausted my mind pouring over concepts of just how this could all be possible. I stepped up out of the car a little after 8 am. I walked over to the Tent area to wake up my two friends I had brought with me. When I got to the tent I had noticed mud on the zipper that opened the tent cover itself. There looked like a faint print of a huge finger on the front cover of the tent opening. I found that to be very odd. I yelled for my friends to wake up. That it was time to get at it. They woke shortly after and came outside.

I quickly showed Bart the muddy print on the tent and he freaked out. I then told him about how rocks were thrown my way as I fished in total darkness back off of the trail. We packed up immediately and set out for home. The trip being cut short out of fear yet once again.

On the way home I was daydreaming constantly. I had all of these interactions with these creatures. But never would they reveal themselves to me in any way. What I hadn't known at the time was that it was coming. And when it finally would take place it would be totally life-changing from that moment forward.

It would happen so many different times it seemed. When I would decide to take an irregular trip to a different location to fish. That was when these encounters had occurred for the most part. I had looked back at my past. For anything that I had done that possibly could have changed the situation. And possibly caused these things to happen.

It was when I took an odd trip out was when these encounters had happened. The next wild encounter I would have was while fishing a Bass Tournament deep down in Louisville Kentucky. My Uncle Jack and I had set out early to win this tournament together. It was supposed to be a Father and Son expedition. And I had to agree to go a week earlier.

We lied, of course, saying he was my father. My Uncle Mike Lilly had taken his son Mike Jr. With him to this tournament as well. Giving us the wrong directions from the start. I would never forget this outing ever. A couple of wild things had taken place that day. At about the halfway point to the lake, we had become lost.

Stopping at an old house deep in the countryside. We were intending on asking for directions. The old man who came out was kind. He gave us simple directions on how to get to Elmer Davis Lake. My Uncle Jack had seen his lake off to the right of us. He asked the old man if there were any big fish in the lake. The old man replied quickly "there may be one or two big ones in there". "No more than that," he said. My Uncle asked him if he could cast a bait out and try to catch one real quick before we left. The old man replied back. "Well have at it". My Uncle grabbed a pole and put on a piece of bait.

Ten minutes later he had hooked the biggest fish I'd ever seen. A huge Flathead or Shovelhead catfish. Weighing well over 40 plus pounds. This thing was a monster no doubt about it. He quickly bulldogged the fish in I netted it and we were off and on our way to the Tournament.

We finally arrived at Elmer Davis Lake. Well over the halfway point of the tournament. The rain began to come down lightly as we backed the boat into the water. Jack turned on the ignition and fired the motor up. We took off towards the other side of the lake. Upon our arrival, we both started to Bass fish.

We were having trouble from the start. The wind was now blowing also. So we knew that would make the fish go deeper automatically. We talked for a few moments before deciding on hitting some small coves well off of the lake. The weather had put us in a pinch quickly. Not knowing of what else to do we hit a small cove.

The wind calmed down as we entered the small area. Just big enough for a boat we started to fish once again. Off the bat, in the first cast, Jack caught a good Bass. We weighed it and measured it. It was a keeper, a good 4-pound fish. Then I threw out a minnow on a slip bobber. Setting it for 2 feet deep.

A few minutes passed by and boom out of nowhere my bobber went under as it floated by a tree in the water. I fought it quickly trying to get it in the boat. We measured it and weighed it quickly. A keeper just under 3 pounds. The fish had seemed to all traveled over and into this very same cove, we were now fishing.

We continued to fish for a couple of more hours in the spot we'd found. The cove itself was only 2 feet deep so it was easy to see to the bottom of the lake. My Uncle was now sight fishing for the bigger females. When I noticed over to the left of me another pocket that had a trail cut into it.

It went back a ways, and then the trail led up to a small mountain on the back side of the trailhead. Deeply forested this place was dense as I'd ever seen an area. Packed with trees and bushes thickets etc. The rain had slowed to a sprinkle. The wind slowed as well. We had almost caught our limit. Jack hooked the last fish about an hour before the tournament had ended.

As we began to measure it and weigh it. We heard it. From the top of the small mountainside. That howl, that blood-curdling sound. So intense that it would rattle your chest. In which It had rattled mine intensely. The sound was so loud it had me totally in fear. I was scared to death at this point. I'd only heard this on audio recordings.

But now I was hearing it as plain as day. On a boat, out in the middle of a lake in the middle of Louisville Kentucky. What a scary end to this whole ordeal was my thought. I asked my Uncle quickly. "Was that a wolf ?" He quickly replied back to me. "No that wasn't a wolf kiddo". "Now we got our limit" "let's get out of here and go weigh in".

We went immediately over to the weigh-in station before we ran out of time. We weighed our fish, and in total had a limit of 5 fish weighing just under 27 pounds. Easily winning the tournament by 8 pounds or a little more. The trophy we received was huge. Well over 3 feet tall and was trimmed in gold.

I will never forget how proud I felt on that day. In that moment I was glorified by this going down the way that it had gone. We had taken first place and beat many good teams on that day. So many people had entered the tournament on that weekend. And at the last moment.

How we managed to come in late 2 hours behind everyone else. And still had won the whole damn thing was a miracle within itself. We packed up the trophy and made sure it didn't get broken on the way home. We got in the truck and made our way to the highway. As soon as we hit the lateral my Uncle looks over to me and says.

"What do you think that was on that mountain Jr." I reply "may be a Bigfoot". He immediately says "Yes" and "your right on the money". I could not believe what we had just heard. It was the most frightening sound I'd ever heard in my life. It had changed my whole perspective on these creatures once again.

I had thought for a moment that maybe the howl that had come from up above us that late in the afternoon hours was that of a Wolf or a Coyote even. That was what I'd hoped it was. But that particular howl was just too damn powerful for it to be any other animal of the forest.

My Uncle educated me basically all of the ways home that evening. About the Myth of the woods that he had actually encountered several times as well while hunting and fishing all over the States of our country. He had told me stories of being paralleled. Ran up into trees on several occasions. While out on hunting expeditions in Arkansas and West Virginia.

He knew that they existed. He had told me all about his trips. How he'd upset something while out hunting and on more than one occasion also. Having the living daylights scared out of you. Being afraid to even attempt to come down and flee the area. At least not until the sun had risen once again.

At this point, I was well past needing the stories to be convinced that these Creatures existed. Too much had happened to me. I was well aware of what was out there. I just hadn't had a full-on encounter as of yet. It was coming sooner than later though. The stars were aligning for this great encounter to take place. Everything about this next event would be set up perfectly to go down the way that it had happened. It would feel as if my life had actually peaked at that moment. Very hard to describe the feeling. It felt as if I had died and been sent to another planet. It was the weirdest feeling I'd ever felt in my life.

That trip up that Mountain that day was an intense climb. Almost straight up and straight down. You had to be experienced to get your ass up to the top. Not just anyone could make that climb. Without gear, it was a hard-ass climb up to the top. Double the trouble with gear on your back. Almost making it impossible. Looking back on the whole situation. I kept going back to each and every moment. Every single detail I had noticed that day. It was most definitely a crazy ass setup. Seeing tree structures as we climbed up towards the top. Seeing several dead deer laying on the right side that sloped down to the Miami White Water River.

One deer had its neck broken and twisted backward. Not a sight for anyone to see, let alone a child. We would learn later that following morning that this had had going on for a while now. I remember back getting to the top of that mountain and throwing my gear down and trying to regain my air back again.

I was so excited though to finally be up to the top. I knew the fishing would be so good. It always was epic. That's the only way that we could describe it. This was one of the best fishing trips we'd decided to take. I was stoked from the moment I reached the top. Never had I ever felt that excited, since the birth of my firstborn son.

I was with my family. My Father and My two Uncles Mike and Rocky Lilly. They were excited as well. We loved it up there on the top of that mountain. We were at peace up there. Felt like Kings sometimes even I think after making that hellacious climb up. Anyone would feel like a King after making that climb.

Everyone got their shit together and we started to fish our butts off. We all had our own special spots to fish. And we all knew how to fish them very well. The day was awesome. We burnt the fish up the whole day. It was late September and a very beautiful day out. Crisp clear blue sky the whole afternoon what a day. The evening rolled in on us and we all prepared for the nighttime Crappie fish with minnows. We knew a spot where the Crappie went deep down into an underwater tree. We would rig up a slip bobber system and set the depth for about 5 feet deep. We knew how to fish in this lake. Lake 1 was a great place to just come and unwind.

Lake 2 was Just another 100 yards or so up the North face of Toms Mountain. The deal was that by the time you made the finish up to the top of lake 1 you were good. No one ever made it to Lake 2 to fish. We were fine right where we were at. And we were ready to fish like we were in a tournament. That's how we were very competitive my Family.

The Cows were crowding the left side of the lake. They loved the shade trees on that side of the lake. I couldn't get to my spot. I was OK though I would wait them out. They were always up there with us on our day trips. This was our first night trip though. I could always walk around the right side of the lake was what I figured on doing if need be.

It was just steep on that side and it sloped down right from the turn. So you had to be careful in the daytime when fishing that side. Let alone the night you would have to be very careful. I would just stay put and fish where I was at for now. It didn't bother me at all. I was in heaven while I was up there.

It was the closest I ever felt to heaven. Even church didn't give me this feeling. Nowhere close to it. I was in my zone up there that was the only thing I knew to be true. The lake sat in a perfect bowl. No wind would come through where we were. There was a ridge to our left that climbed up and wrapped around to lake 2. Keeping it secluded just out of reach of our eyesight.

The Northside was just a grassy climb up a good hundred yards further. To our right was a muddy and grassy slope down to the river which flowed so strongly that you could hear it at the top of the lake. It was so calming almost hypnotizing in a sense. It was a perfect setup for anything to live and thrive up there at the top of this mountain.

Everything could be seen while we were up there. Cows, Deer, Fox, Rabbits, Squirrels, Birds, etc. You name it we were among it while we were up there. It was such a wonderful feeling to be free from all of the stress and anxiety of the world brought on by everyday life. Being there was an escape for all of us.
At nightfall, something seemed to change the whole top of the Mountain. The mood seemed to be that of panic. Everything went totally silent at dark as the sun set to the West. The whole area seemed to change in just a few moment's time. I thought nothing of it and just kept on fishing. It was in the back of my mind though.
The night began to cool down from the long warm day that we'd had. We all put on our Hoodies And continued to fish well into the night hours. At about 12 midnight all life seemed to stop showing any signs of its existence. The Cows even got up and

took off on us. Moving around to the right side of the lake.
Making their move towards lake number 2. We thought that to
be kind of strange. I watched as they made their climb up. I was
kind of shocked to see them go actually. They had usually stuck
by our side the whole time we were there. I shook it off and just
continued to fish. Deep down I was starting to think about the
possibilities of something wild taking place.

The fog came rolling up the hill from down off of the river below.
It became a little freaky at that moment I can't lie. I was actually
pretty scared. I'd never been up at Toms during the night ever.
This was the first time that anyone had ever been up here at
night and It was quite a scene, a sight for sore eyes. But we were
on edge. All of us were I'd have to say.

It was at about a half hour after the Cows had left the area that
we had first heard the sounds come from atop of the ridge way
up towards the top. The ridge sat on the left side of the lake. We
were all in the middle at this point. I hadn't even tried to move to
my spot yet. The crappies were hitting right where we were at.
I had heard it first. Since I was the closest to the ridge. It was a
Deer was what I had first thought. So I reported it back over to
my family quietly to not spook the fish. And we shook it off and
continued to fish through the situation. Every so often it sounded

as if this deer just kept on creeping closer to us. So evasively and defensively down towards our location.

We fished on and on through the night hours having fun and thinking nothing of what we had heard over on the left ridge just a while back some time ago. We had thought nothing more of it. We had no clue at all what was getting ready to take place. It was like something out of a scene shooting for a movie. But this wasn't the case here at all.

My Uncle Mike told everyone to quiet down as we were talking and having fun. He had heard something he said over off to the left side of the lake. He said it sounded like a newborn baby whining out. I said to him "No Way In Hell". "Were up on a mountain top". Then we all heard it whine out again, just vaguely. I started to freak out right there at that moment. Thinking what could this really be? There was no way in Hell that there was a baby up here with us! It was not possible. Or was it? What had we just heard? Then it let out another whine out of nowhere. It sounded just like a baby there was no doubt about it at all.

My Uncle asked me to make the walk over to the left side and see what I could get my eyes on. I was very hesitant about moving anywhere near the left side of the lake at the time. I thought to myself if I find a baby over there I'm going to flip out.

That had me very nervous I was really weighing my options at that point in time.

As I built up the courage to even attempt the walk over to that side of the lake. I made sure that I had grabbed the Lantern. I needed to be able to see what exactly it was and I needed to see where I was at as well. I didn't want to fall in the lake. It was getting very cold outside as the early morning hours rolled in. It was now about 4 am, or a little after.

I slowly made the walk over towards the left side of the lake. As I got to the turn I slowly raised the light up to be able to see clearly. I wanted to be sure without a doubt what It was I looking at. As I turned the corner I slipped a little bit in the mud. The turn was a tight one. The woods were so close to the water on the left side of the lake. You had to be careful on that side. There was only a 3-foot-wide path carved out.

As I caught my balance I pushed forward to see what was now just feet away. I raised up the lantern once again and put light right on a huge being. As I did it raised its right hand out of the water slowly. The water could be seen dripping off its hand. I was instantly frozen with fear. I couldn't even move a muscle at the moment.

It was in that moment that my life changed FOREVER. For now, what was in front of me want possibly human. That was my first thought upon seeing this creature in a squatted position. Next to the lake grabbing a drink of water as if it were resting. On two legs clearly a bipedal creature. Huge feet, very impressive build this thing had to it. All muscles for the most part.

I was in shock as I could barely hear my Uncle ask me whispering softly. "Jr., what is that"? "Do you see that"? He got no answer from me. I was in a trance at the moment. Almost as if I had been hypnotized. I stood there trying to break down this creature's body. To make sure just what in the hell it was that I was looking at.

The stories were all true. I knew now without a doubt that there were more than one of these beasts roaming about. I just couldn't believe what I was seeing. What they say is true. Your mind begins to try and make sense of it all. Your brain is trying to comprehend all of the information it is receiving.

What I was looking at was about 7 and a half feet tall easily. It weighed about 450 to 500 pounds. It was a huge man-like beast with a very broad chest and fur or hair all about its body. Its arms were very long as well. Its skin was a dark tan from what I could see. This thing was impressive. As it slowly turned its head my way as I heard a low rumbling guttural growl grow in intensity. Its eyes glowed a beautiful shade of yellow off of the lantern light. Its head was huge as the top of it seemed to be a peak which was wild to me. The muscles on this beast's body were intense as they bulged out as if he were a professional linebacker from a football team. There were no breasts on this creature like in the patty video. Not as big as the one I'd seen as a young kid. The legs were longer than a normal human being. The teeth were even bigger than a humans as well. Every single body part was exceptionally bigger than that of any human I'd ever seen before. That was the shocking part that froze me as I looked for detail after detail to make sure what I was seeing. I didn't want to make any mistake of this being a bear or anything else.

And there was no doubt about it. This wicked but beautiful creature was not a bear or wolf or Coyote either. It was a Sasquatch there was no doubt about it. This one had to of come across the water to get to where we were. The reason I say this is because there was no smell to this thing unless I missed it out of fear or the shock of the whole situation had got the best of me. On being able to bring that detail forward.
The fact that I was seeing this had been confirmed there in those very few short moments. I had paid full attention to detail. What had me shook was how in the hell hadn't anyone else seen this creature. Surely they would have warned us if they had seen it. I

thought for sure Tom would have at least seen it. Hell, he lived here; this was his land.

He would have warned us for sure if he'd in fact known that this thing was here. I'm now slowly coming to. But I'm still locked in on this wicked half human half ape-like creature. It is staring back at me now at this time as well. It's looking at me and then glances over to the woods just off to its left like it wants to bolt and take off.

But in fact, it doesn't move. It stays put for a while longer. When I glance over towards the woods where it's looking to run. I see a baby doe, a baby deer locked in this creature's left hand. By the neck, it has it in its grasp. And it's locked on like a vice grip. The poor animal was not going anywhere. It was doomed that was one thing that was for sure.

I vaguely hear my Family whispering over my way. "Jr., do you see that? What is that?" I continue to stare at this thing for a few more seconds before turning to run away for my safety. It was continuing to growl at me in an aggressive manner. I could see why though honestly. It had captured its hunt and was protecting it. As the baby Deer kicked its legs frantically about trying to free itself.

I know that I would do the same exact thing if I had just spent all that time stalking and hunting an animal. Only to have someone come across maybe trying to steal your hunt from you. That would be enough to cause a standoff. I was only hoping that wasn't was this was. If so I was in grave danger. The danger of being put in a grave if I messed with this thing at all. That was my thought exactly.

I knew it was time to leave. As I turned to run I yell over to my Family to take off and now. To go and jump if need be in order to get away from this thing. Maybe there were more than one of these things roaming about the area. It was really time to get out of there. I was now running towards the side of the Mountain. I hit the side and jumped over and down towards the slope. As I hit the ground I was running. That's how scared I was of the situation. I was now in fear for my life for sure. I wasn't sure if we all would make it through this moment. I remember looking back as I jumped off of the edge. The creature was still stuck it seemed like a Deer stuck in headlights.

Unable to move it seemed. Most likely it was just protecting its hunt. That's what I thought for the most part. The whole situation was just an uncomfortable one for me. I'd seen something that was not of this world. At least that was what I had been told my entire life. And now I had definitely seen otherwise with no doubts at all.

We were all now running down off of the side of this mountain. Possibly our lives are in danger at this time. The situation had just changed for the worst. I was out in front trying to lead the way as I shined the lantern up to give light to be able to see in which direction to go. As I raised the light I slowed down a little bit.

That got me taken out from behind as all of our legs had all become entangled as my Father and Uncles had been right on my ass the whole time. They were just as afraid as I was of this thing. It was easy to see why they were afraid of this creature. I know I was totally in fear at this time.

As we all hit the ground we rolled and tumbled end over end. Crashing into huge boulders and downed trees and limbs. Getting ripped and scraped up as we slowly made our way down the mountainside. I was looking back constantly to see if this beast was anywhere behind us. I had the feeling that many sets of eyes were now on us.

We had been very fortunate the Sasquatch had not Chased us. But I still felt scared to death. As if my life were in Jeopardy for some reason. I don't know why I felt that way. Just then I stopped tumbling downward I had landed next to a huge tree that had fallen to the ground. I quickly tried to get up and continue to run again.

But for some reason, I had no use of my legs at this point in time. I couldn't move a muscle. Fear or some other form of energy had taken the use of my limbs from me. I couldn't move my body and now fear had overwhelmed me. My whole life started to flash before my eyes. As I began to think that this was the end. That this beast was coming to kill us all. The feeling of doom now consumed me instantly.

It was in those few moments that I started to pray to the Lord. To save us from this situation we were enduring. My Family had all landed right next to me. Shortly behind me not too far off. We all were experiencing the same thing. None of us could move for about 5 minutes. It was very strange to be so afraid that we couldn't move. What was happening to me I thought to myself. Why in the hell can I not move?

I remember feeling so scared and yet so hopeless at the same time. It was the most empty feeling I'd ever felt in my life ever. And I had been through some very scary shit in my lifetime. Finally, after 5 minutes time, we were able to get up and move. Struggling to get down to the bottom of the hill.

The terrain was steep and rugged, especially in the pitch Black darkness. We struggled to make it down to the bottom of the mountain. After about 20 minutes of struggling to get down off of the hillside, we had finally made it to the bottom and at Tom's parking lot. We were winded and trying to catch our breath. I was so emotional at that moment. But then as quickly as we had arrived my Uncle pulled us all together in a group. Telling me to keep all of what just had transpired a secret. That if this were to get out around the city. That people would be out on Tom's land trying to hunt these things down. Causing all hell to break loose.

I knew if there was a juvenile up there. There had to be more of them up there. There was no doubt in my mind. I knew it from the moment I'd seen the juvenile Sasquatch that there had to be more of them living up there. So in a sense, I knew deep down that my Uncle Mike was totally right. So it was then decided. If it got out that we'd seen a Sasquatch up on that Mountain. People would flock to that location fully loaded with their guns blazing. So I had to really dig down deep and suppress the whole damn encounter from beginning to end. It really had me flustered at that moment. Tom had overheard all of the commotion going on.

He came out on the porch and asked us if we were OK. My Uncle Mike started to tell him what was going on. The neighbor next door came shortly after. Asking if everything was alright. We had to tell them honestly for their safety. My Uncle Mike was talking to Tom as I talked to the neighbor. I told him what we'd seen. He immediately called 911 and a State Trooper arrived soon after. Come to find out they had a feeling something was off about their land as of late. They had both talked to us about finding dead Deer on their land. Some of them had been ripped apart. And some had even had their necks broken and twisted backward. Which really had Tom and his neighbor freaking out as of late. The neighbor seemed to be excited at what I'd witnessed. Saying he'd had the feeling all along.

The State Trooper asked me what it was I'd seen. I explained it the best I could at that time to him. He suggested right off of the bat that No one go back up there for a while. He'd told us that they had recently been getting a lot of calls lately about encounters in the area. Near the Miami White Water River area. We agreed with him that it wouldn't be safe to go up there at this time. That was for sure. I told him that it had hunted down a baby Deer. So it may be dangerous to go up there honestly. Everyone agreed and Tom was shocked to find out what we had witnessed up on his lake. It was definitely a game changer for all of us.

We all talked for several more minutes to the State Policeman about the encounter. What I'd noticed though immediately he wasn't taking our statement seriously at all. He wasn't writing it down. As if he felt like someone would look at him differently or ridicule him for even taking down our information at the time. He seemed to be interested though in what had transpired up there. As he gave us his full attention during our conversation. He was freaked out a little himself it seemed to be as he said. "I don't think that I'd be very comfortable going up there by myself, especially during the nighttime hours".

We all agreed in an instant that it wouldn't be wise at all to even attempt a climb up the dark. For one it was a hell of a climb during the daytime. Let alone trying to attempt the climb up in the darkness. It was just too dangerous. We had told him that all of our fishing gear was still up on top of the Mountains.

We didn't want to lose any of it if that were at all possible. But we were totally helpless because of the situation that had occurred. We would have to wait until the sun rose once again. Then maybe it would be safe to go back up and grab our fishing gear. That was what we all agreed on as we got in the car to make the long drive home.

We told Tom to be safe as we all packed in the car, saying our goodbyes as we pulled out of his parking lot. We then started to make the drive back towards Cincinnati which was only about a 40-minute drive from where we were. I believe that was the most shocking for me. To now know that this species truly existed.

And that they were living not too far out of reach from mankind. Just beyond the city limits in the forest on top of a small mountain. I was changed from that moment forward. Having to struggle with what I had just witnessed with my Family. Just outside of our hometown. Not too far from home that was the crazy part about this whole situation.

My Uncle went back the next day and grabbed our gear. Armed of course for his own protection. The sad part was that I never went back there and fished ever again. It had me scared to even attempt to go back into the woods. I didn't sigh for many years after this encounter. Finally, after telling my story, I went on one fishing trip with my brother Jason during the daytime shortly before he passed away.

He and I and a good friend of ours Billy Gunkle had gone fishing at a section of the Little Miami River. Not too far from home. We had a great time that day. As I explained to them I had just released my book about my true encounter while up on Toms. They were both shocked when I told them what I had seen. My brother passed away shortly after this trip and it really affected me tremendously. As I had arrived too late to even attempt to save his life. It had taken me well over 20 years to be able to let all of this information out. Afraid of being ridiculed by others. After a life-changing event had taken place. I decided that it was time to come clean with what id witnessed.

And allow my soul to heal finally after all of these years had gone by. My life never to be the same ever again. So I hope that everyone enjoys this book as it all unfolds. You will picture the fear that we had all been put through on that night. Such a frightening thing to experience. Even with others being present it was still so scary and yet shocking.

Shortly after releasing my books about my encounters. I went live on several Bigfoot shows and talked about my encounter. I even went as far as presenting my encounters to several Organizations. Sasquatch Theory, Cryptids Canada, Buckeye Bigfoot, and my good buddy over on Old bears Den. As well as telling my story to The Skookum Report.

There are several videos now out there about all of my encounters. On those channels. Or you can just read my books. They are very educational for the most part. But also a bit frightening as well I must say. So I hope whoever reads this enjoys it. And I also hope it helps educate others who aren't familiar with this subject matter.

Now after I had finished several projects. Releasing my first two books. A friend and I had decided to take a vacation and head down to his mother and father's land In Kentucky. We were going to fish at Laurel Lake. We left on a Friday and the goal was to get some good fishing in over the weekend.

We arrived late during the night hours on early Saturday morning. We pulled in and the land was beautiful. Two houses sat side by side and woods surrounded the whole area beyond their homes. We chatted a while with Johnathan my good friend Tim's little brother. And then grabbed a couple of hours' sleep. Waking up at about 7 we ate some good Blueberries for breakfast and had some powerful coffee. Then we headed over to wake up Tim's dad John. We needed to get him up and then put together our fishing gear. On the way over to John and Judy's house. Tim looks down and finds a Deer leg. Right in the middle of the field leading to his Mom and dad's house.

He picks it up and says to me. "Jeff" "look at this man". He hands it to me as I begin to look at this huge leg. It had been twisted and twisted over and over again until it had popped off of the body and separated. Now we both look at one another. And just shake our heads in shock. This wasn't a normal thing to see at all. Not in this area, out in an open field!

Now Tim knew that I had just put out a couple of Books about Sasquatch and my life's encounters. Now he was becoming intrigued by what we had just found. He couldn't believe what he'd seen. Right next to his Mom and Dad's house. I took pictures of it and put them on Facebook immediately for others to see. We then walked over to the Deck and placed the leg on the table. Tim went to wake his dad as I started putting fishing poles together. John comes out and Tim shows him the Deer leg instantly. John looks at it and says "Wow, what in the hell was able to this kind of damage to a Deer"? "Surely not something a Coyote could do".

The leg looked like it had just been wrung out like wet clothing. John sat the leg down on the table and we say nothing more about it. We get the gear together and hitch the boat up to the truck and head down towards the Lake. It had started to sprinkle the rain as we arrived at the boat ramp.

I get out of the truck to help John back the boat in. As I hit the back of the boat next to the lake itself. Something was thrown my way from up off of the ridge up above me about a hundred feet. I looked down to find what was thrown at me and couldn't find what was thrown my way. I was spooked as my senses were put on high alert at that moment.

I think nothing more of it as I start to try and help guide John to the water. We finally get the boat backed up perfectly as we all

jump in the boat. John drives the truck up and around to the

parking lot and walks back down the hill and jumps in with us.

Tim starts the motor up and we set out to fish the opposite side

of the boats that were tubing.

Once we'd arrive at the other side of the lake. We dropped the

boat anchor. As we started to fish the boats started rolling by

heavy. On the opposite side of the lake from us. It was in that

moment that they must have upset something just up a ways in

the wood line. We continued to try and fish as the waves rolled

in smacking the boat and pushing us left to right.

Just then we all heard a tree falling from the other side of the

lake. The tree had been clearly pushed over you could hear it

snapping and cracking right before popping and smacking the

ground. It sounded like a cruise missile hitting the ground. We

were all so shocked that we jumped up off of the boat as it

floated in the water.

We were all in shock as the tree crashed into the ground. Tim

looks at me and says "Wow" "this trips getting interesting

already" as he laughs. I'm in shock once again as I know most

likely what had caused that tree to get knocked over. We let it go

and start to fish some more.

An hour later we get hit with a major thunderstorm. Trying to find our way back to the boat dock. To get to safety and pull the boat out before we get struck by lightning. The whole time I feel as if we got eyes on us the whole damn time. We had been in a cove just a few moments earlier.

I took pictures of the area. It was paved so beautifully with huge flat rocks. Looking as if it had been carved to have that look. The woods were thick with sets of huge trees. Pines and Maples and Ash spread all about the area perfectly. While we were in that cove the hair on my neck and arms had stood straight up as I felt that wild feeling come over me once again out of nowhere.

I finally talked them out of the cove and back towards the dock. We hitched the boat up and headed back to the house. We finished the day exploring Tim's parent's land. They had a natural spring-fed pond down from the houses. It sat about 3 hundred yards away and was surrounded by thick woods. Packed with Deer ticks. As I would find out several days later.

We figured that's where the killing of that Deer had to of taken place. We fished for a couple of hours at the pond. Catching huge Bluegill. The rain rolled in again pushing us back to the house quickly. We finished our trip the next morning and said our goodbyes. It was hard I hadn't seen them in years. They were my second family. And I loved them deeply and would miss them.

We packed our stuff and headed out towards Ohio. Rolling through each town while on the local Highway. What happened next was so shocking. It had me really thinking about the things we'd experienced while at Tim's parents. We rolled into Berea Kentucky as the rain started falling heavily slowing us down.

I look over to the right side of the Highway. What I see is a huge hill, climbing up to a mountain top. The top of this mountain had been Stripped of every single tree. Flattened out to pave and make way for a new section of road or Highway. So much equipment was on top of that huge mountain top. I just couldn't believe they had Stripped that much forest away.

When out of nowhere Tim yells over at me. "Hey check this shit out" Jeff. And as I look over at him. We are now seeing tree breaks all along this stretch of Highway just on the opposite side from the construction site project. As if something were letting out its anger. Down a stretch of about a hundred yards. Along a set path of destruction. The clean and clear tree breaks at 7 to 7 and a half feet high.

We both look at each other as Tim says, "Well we learned a whole lot more while being down here". I agree immediately with him, "There is no doubt about it". We had learned so much more on this trip. It was our belief that the Sasquatch in the area had been upset. In such ways, they were pushing over trees and making tree breaks.

Letting it be known that they were angry as they were marking new territory. It was the only way we could process what we had on our minds at that time. It totally made sense. The tree breaks in a straight line down a stretch of Highway. The opposite side of a new road build. Trees being pushed over just down the road a ways at a lake.

It was our belief that these creatures were acting out. Over their woods being Stripped away from them. Pushing them down off of the mountainside. To the other side of the woods. Or pushing them down towards the Lake area. And they were truly showing their anger in several different ways now for sure.

We had experienced so many things that couldn't all be explained away. The Deer leg being twisted off of a body. As if it were a wet piece of clothing being wrung out while soaked. The huge tree that had been pushed over while we were fishing the lake. The tree breaks all along the Highway. Across from a new road build. The incident of something being thrown at me from up on a ridge beside a lake.

There had been simply too many damn incidents taking place during our trip. They couldn't all be explained away. It was that simple. Everything that was going on down there at the time may have just upset the balance of their world. And we were just lucky enough to be in the right place at the right time. That was my outlook on the situation.

That whole area is nothing but woods. Everywhere you look is all forest. Plenty of places for this species to hide and thrive. Away from humans. There have been so many encounters and sightings down in the State of Kentucky. I've not had the privilege of seeing one. But have had several incidents that cannot be explained away.

Let me just say this. I know that they are roaming about down in the hills and mountains of Kentucky. I've seen footprints recently. As well as so many other pieces of evidence. That has been captured by several researchers that I know and work with. Most of us who spend a lot of time in the woods, know truthfully what it is that's out there.

I have no doubt about it after all of the things that I have seen while out there living life my way. I've been very fortunate to have had several sightings and encounters during my life. My only hope is that once the species has been proven. I hope mankind doesn't do anything to destroy this special breed of creature.

It has taken me well over 25 years of fishing and hunting and witnessing These Hybrid Humans while out doing the things that I enjoy deeply. One can't simply ignore all of the videos and pictures. As well as the 1000's of reports of encounters. You simply have to go out and enjoy the woods and forests across the country to have a chance of an encounter.

The more time you spend out in those areas. The better the chance you have. To witness a creature of this kind. And If you're lucky enough to have an encounter you too will then experience the same thought process that so many others have gone through while coming across this Mythical beast.

The fact that so many people are ridiculed over having a sighting or an encounter is truly sad. I believe that is why we are so far behind when it comes to knowing more about the subject of Sasquatch. That is the one thing that keeps so many others who have had an encounter or sighting from coming forward.

I look at it now and think to myself. Just how many more stories are out there that we know nothing about. Because of the ridicule that others are so afraid to experience. After telling about their own encounter to others. Which is the one thing that keeps so many other stories from coming to the light.

To me, that would seem to possibly double the numbers of

sightings themselves maybe even tripling them all together. Making the subject of Sasquatch all that more exciting for the ones who do Research on a daily basis. The work is being done in order to prove the existence of this special species of Hybrid Human.

I dedicate this book to those who love the subject that I write about. And as well as my friends and family. The truth is out there! Some of us get lucky enough to witness these beautiful Hybrid Hominids in action. The more you're in the woods with nature the better your chances are.

As of late, there are very many sightings going down in the State of Kentucky. As well as Ohio. These are the peak months when they are spotted during the night hours. From June on through October are the prime months for an encounter or sighting. Usually while driving. Or out fishing or camping as well.

Or at a local or State Park as well. While Camping or Fishing. These are prime times for a possible interaction with this special group of species. The Research and proof of its existence have come a very long way. And has been proven to many that they do indeed exist. Only to be shunned away by others who simply don't believe.

I'm so glad that I spent so much time out in the woods when I was growing up. It paved the road for me to be able to see the things I was able to witness. And had truly changed my life forever during that first sighting. Even though my experiences came to me in the way that seemed to be a build-up. Almost as if I were being slowly brought to this reality.

It still affected me so greatly that I wasn't totally prepared for it to take place. It spun my whole world around as if it were on an axis. And I had to learn how to live with the fact that I'd seen what I'd seen and couldn't undo it. Once you see something you can't unsee it. And that is how it goes. I struggled with so many issues after my encounters.

I had kept these Encounters to myself for well over 20 years. Before deciding to let go of them. Allowing myself to finally heal after all of the trauma I had seen over the years. I hope this book helps others to just let go and tell their story. No matter the ridicule or outcome. Allow yourself to come to peace with what you've seen. That's the most important part of an encounter. Once one has happened you will find yourself going back over the encounter time and time again. Trying to make sense of it all. I was told to keep our encounter a secret in order to keep what we had seen up there safe. So others wouldn't be up there in a frenzy. Trying to hunt and kill just How many ever of these creatures that may have been up there living and thriving.

Looking back now on my past. I feel as if the encounters I'd had were for the most part meant to be. I can honestly say that I was stone-cold sober and well aware of my surroundings. During each and every encounter that I had. I do feel now after doing years of research and studying the phenomenon.

I believe they are honestly drawn to certain people. People that have a special kind of soul. A pure soul, a clean soul. People who are at peace while in the woods and forests. Souls of certain People who aren't evil. But loving and sincere people. People as well who give off a certain kind of vibe or energy. Those who wouldn't hurt a soul.

Those special kinds of people to me would be the ones who are blessed while out in the woods and forests. To actually get an encounter or even a sighting. I feel as if I am honestly one of those people. Being born an identical twin and losing my brother in the process. I grew and became more loving as I aged.

Being kind and caring to all of those around me. Helping others as much as I could. And in any way that I possibly could. I feel as if that were the reason for me being interacted with many times while out deep in the woods. At several different locations. I don't believe that it is the equation of being at the right place at the right time for some people.

Those who have multiple encounters over the duration of their life. This I believe happens because of the person themselves is a genuine and loving soul. I do believe however that many others have encounters while out driving the roads of the United States. During certain hours of the day and nights as well.

I've had enough time out in the woods and forest that makes me more than just your so-called average couch researcher so to speak. My last outing down to Laurel Lake deep down in Kentucky. Was a very educating trip for me. As you read earlier in the book. The fact that something had been clearly pushed off of the mountainside.
And had let out its stress by causing tree breaks down along a section of Highway on the opposite side of where their build was taking place. It was actually shocking to see those breaks on a stretch and in a straight line for about a hundred yards. Along with the twisted-off Deer leg. That was also very shocking for me to see.
Along with having thrown at me just off of the ridge above me at the boat ramp that rainy day. Was freaky as well. The huge tree being pushed over was the most shocking to me. It just wasn't a normal situation for one to experience. I had never had a tree fall near me anywhere while in the woods.
It seemed as if something had been upset by all of the boat

traffic that was taking place on that side of the lake that day. And it made it known that it was upset. Just too many things to explain away as being all just a simple coincidence. There was no way anyone could tell me otherwise. I knew better this wasn't m first rodeo after all.

I've had too many rock-throwing incidents alone to be explained away. As well as two up and close very personal encounters with these special creatures. One I believe was a freak mishap. I believe the first encounter happened because the Hybrid had become lost. In my last encounter, I believe that we were in the right place at the right time.
Being down on the flat bowl-like surface of lake 1 that night. I believe that the second sighting of the juvenile happened because he couldn't smell us as we were downwind from it the whole damn time until the very end of his hunt. When I walked up on him with a baby doe in his grasp. I believe it was at that moment that he let out that snort.
At the very end of his growl, as if he were disgusted almost. That he'd been seen while on his hunt. Which was very unexpected and seemed to have had him just as shocked as I was at that time. It was totally life-changing for me as we both stood there in disbelief of our situation at hand.

The End

(Written By Jeffrey Lilly Jr)

The Night The Stars Aligned

by

Jeffrey Lilly Jr

Author Bio

Jeffrey David Lilly Jr has spent more than 20 years in the field of bigfoot study. He has logged countless hours reviewing alleged bigfoot videos as well as talking to numerous first hand account witnesses. Jeffrey also enjoys taking time to fishing, hunting and to go camping. He currently resides in Ohio.

Look for these other great titles from Zombie Media

Bigfoot and Steller Jay's River Day

The Leaf Lady at the Amber Estates

True Short Stories of the Paranormal: My Personal Experiences

The Adventures of Pete Johnson and the Ghosts of Scott's

Mountain

Understanding Bigfoot

Bigfoot Witness

My Haunted House and other Weird Tales

I saw a UFO: Mysteries of the sky

Bigfoot and Eastern Cousins

Sasquatch Family Ties

The Ivory-billed Woodpecker:Taunting Extinction

Available on Amazon and other fine retailers

www.ingramcontent.com/pod-product-compliance
Lightning Source LLC
Chambersburg PA
CBHW051345150726
48000CB00003B/1057